LET the KiD GUIDE

Putting Nature Back into Our Lives

Margot Angstrom & Lisa Kosglow
Illustrated by Sarah Uhl

gatekeeper press

Let the Kid Guide
Putting Nature Back into Our Lives

Published by Gatekeeper Press
2167 Stringtown Rd, Suite 109
Columbus, OH 43123-2989
www.GatekeeperPress.com

The cover design, interior formatting, typesetting, and editorial work for this book are entirely the product of the author. Gatekeeper Press did not participate in and is not responsible for any aspect of these elements.

Graphic Design by Jodi Hougard Petty

ISBN: 9781642376791 paperback

Safety Note

The activities in this book are intended to be carried out with adult supervision. Risk management and precaution is recommended at all times when exploring outside with children. While this book is intended as an activity guide, please exercise common sense and sound judgement at all times. The authors and publisher disclaim liability for any injury, damage or mishap that may occur from the activities in this book. Bottom-line: "Let the kid guide" within reason, and always play hard, play safe and play smart.

gatekeeper press

To all the guides who strive to
teach, inspire, celebrate and nurture
the children in all of us.

"If a child is to keep alive his inborn sense of wonder, he needs the companionship of at least one adult who can share it, rediscovering with him the joy, excitement and mystery of the world we live in."

~ Rachel Carson

What's Inside

LET the KiD GUIDE

Magic Happens...

...when agendas are set aside, and we follow the moment. This isn't permissive parenting, rather a deep acknowledgement of the inner wisdom contained in children and grown-ups alike. We don't need a lesson plan or an exhaustive gear list - simply, the willingness to open the senses, open the imagination and let the kid guide.

Many guidebooks provide a mass of activities to do outside. These books are useful; our book is different. Through activities, information and personal stories as well as insight from our community in "Collective Wisdom" pages, we aim to help you build an exploration ethic. This book inspires a philosophy on how to relate, motivate and encourage kids and sets a foundation for investigating the world. The approach is inquiry-based and interdisciplinary. Concepts of science, art, mindfulness and primitive skills are incorporated throughout the book in a way that helps adults tap into knowledge and experience they have stored inside them, even if it was switched off long ago.

This re-found sense of wonder helps readers play, connect with one another and embrace not having all the answers. Leading with observation, questioning and gratitude, families learn life skills that will cultivate our leaders for tomorrow. Curiosity, independence, confidence, resilience, empathy -- these are the attributes of the problem-solvers who will guide our future.

Go out, play and discover,

Margot and Lisa

Let's Get Started

Set up for Success and Fun

When I was less experienced with groups, I would enthusiastically announce, "We're hiking today!" Often I was met with groans. While some kids enjoy a hike, many don't. My playfulness is infectious, but also how I preface the day is key to success. I've learned to say, "We're going to the woods to build forts," or "...to the lake to look for salamanders." When I'm more creative I get buy in and the kids... they barely realize they're hiking.

Pack-up Have an accessible bag (by the door or in your car) with the essentials: a towel or picnic blanket, water bottle, snacks, sunscreen, hats, binoculars, a small field guide for your area and field journal tools. These may vary seasonally and as interests change. It's much easier to mobilize if the basics are already packed.

Journal Bring a simple, small field journal and a small pouch with a hand lense, pencil, eraser, some colored pencils, sharpener, a small watercolor set, a few paintbrushes and a glue stick. Make notes, draw pictures, glue in specimens, write stories and list questions for follow-up at home. Not only does it help trigger curiosity and investigation, it becomes a cherished keepsake. Check out Clare Walker Leslie or Hannah Hinchman, our favorite authors on keeping a field journal.

> We try to head out on the early side of the day when my daughter is most energetic. We also try to give her a choice as to where we go exploring. ~ Kevin T.

The Huddle

Whether starting a long day in the woods or a walk to the post office, check-in with the "Team." Get a pulse on basic needs of your group and establish a tone for the activity. Adjust your approach depending on the age, group's size, duration and type of activity. Sometimes it's appropriate to discuss and set guidelines together. Kids have great ideas, and if they help write the rules, they will more likely follow them. In other situations certain rules must be followed. Huddle up with the following four items in mind.

How to Huddle: Turn Groans into Grins

Who Needs What? We've all been there: 10 minutes into an outing you hear, "I have to pee." Get all needs met before you leave: food, water as well as emotional needs. Does her stuffed mouse need to come along for her to feel happy? Great. Bring it.

What's the Weather Like Today? Brief everyone on how to keep safe and comfortable in the day's changing environment: sun protection, appropriate clothing layers and precipitation.

What's the Point? Develop relevance and motivation by reminding everyone the point of it all. Exploring, family time or just having fun are perfect reasons to be out and together.

We're in This Together! Establish a way to keep track of everyone (counting off or buddy system), encourage teamwork and finish with a rousing cheer! Enduring the rain together, my daughter turns and says, "Mom, I'm a rain-deer. Get it?" Yes. She gets it!

The Roots

We can't promise your outing won't inlcude frustration or tears, but we can offer these simple precepts we follow to remind us how to Let the Kid Guide.

1. Be Playful We don't control much in life. What we do control is our attitudes, and how we approach what life throws our way. Find the people that are willing to be playful and positive, happy and humble. Laugh. Joke. Poke fun at yourself. Infuse the epic, mundane, life! with joy.

2. Tune-In Heighten awareness of yourself, your family and the world around you. Observe your surroundings. Ignite your senses to notice sights, sounds, smells, tastes, feelings and attitudes. Be present with your crew. Put phones away. Listen and respond to questions and concerns.

3. Talk Less & Do More Many adults want to teach or talk at their kids, when kids really just want to do things together. Value this special time. Deepen relationships through shared experiences. It's often the experience that teaches best.

4. Answer with Questions Why, you ask? Why not?! Refrain from giving immediate answers. Wait and respond with more questions to encourage independent thinking. This process cultivates curiosity and builds pathways for more learning.

5. Model Wonder & Gratitude Be mindful of your actions; kids learn from what we model. Focus on what's fun for them but also for you. Balance your interests and hobbies with theirs. Your engagement is infectious. Lastly, be generous with gratitude as happiness stems from it.

Collective Wisdom Many of us have a community to share ideas, advice, as well as a laugh at our parenting-fails. When writing *Let the Kid Guide*, we connected with our tribe of experienced educators and creative parents. The Collective Wisdom in the book include nuggets from them and honor the wisdom we all have, even if we can't seem to access it as our child writhes in a temper tantrum, refusing to move another step!

Encourage Questions

Why? Do we have to? When will we get there?

For millennia, from the Socratic to the scientific method, inquiry has stimulated critical thinking, new ideas and ultimately success for the species—as well as complete aggravation for weary parents! Current brain-based research supports inquiry to promote learning. Diving into our brains and sifting through it to recall information or experiences, allows new pathways and connections to be made, while strengthening what is already known. Take a deep breath and embrace the questions.

Observe Start to develop observation skills; use all of your senses. Example: "I notice this tree bark is rough and craggy."

Question Next, dive into the unknown. What makes you curious? Example: "I wonder why this tree has such deep, thick bark?"

Recall Then go deeper; connect to something else. What does it make you think? Example: "This bark reminds me of pictures of the earth taken from the sky."

Side-by-Side Popping off facts is not the point. Rather, continue the questioning with them. Share your own observations, wonders, and connections. Doing so models curiosity and helps everyone learn more.

My daughter, the consummate questioner, automatically fires "Why?" after most comments. It's a habit, often with no real desire to listen to "the why." But sometimes it's different. Sometimes after a pause she'll pursue: "Can we try that?" or "Remember that time when..." or "Did you ever feel that way when you were little?" When she connects to an existing idea, memory or experience, we know it's going to "stick."

Bring on the Weather!

Be ready to play outside in all weather

Embracing the weather is essential to getting outside. Otherwise, we would be stuck inside on most days. The key is to adjust our mindset: every day is a beautiful day and even more so when we begin to explore the out-of-doors irrespective of weather. We must shift our attitudes and our language. Camping on the Oregon coast in March with a three and two-year-old shows our kids' fortitude. They never once balked at the downpours and gale-force winds. They always wanted to get on their scoot-bikes or play in the sand. With proper gear, fuel and attitudes, we can play too.

Wick, Warm & Weather

Find good, technical clothing; share with friends and buy at secondhand stores. Good gear lasts even the intense play of children. An easy layering system to remember while dressing for the out-of-doors, especially during cold or rainy months, includes three layers. The wicking layer is lightweight and draws moisture from your skin into the clothing to keep it from cooling your body temperature. The warmth layer varies depending on the temperature and activity. The last layer protects you from the weather, and depends on the conditions, whether rain, snow or wind. Begin teaching your children this system early. Older children can easily remember these steps, take ownership of the process and be confident in their outerwear choices.

Explore

As you're dressing yourself and your kids, encourage them to think like an animal. What would a fox wear today? Or come up with your own cues, "We need to wear our down feathers today"; "Let's put on our beetle armor"; "It looks like a puddle-stomping day." Reluctant sunscreen wearers? No problem. We "paint" our faces to look like an animal, "Time to put on our whiskers" or scales or feathers, depending on the preferred animal. Or maybe it's an animal attitude you want to inspire in your kids, "Let's go, Storm Kitty," when they are reluctant to get out into the storm or back on the slopes. Collect and post by your "gear-up station" photos of animals in different types of weather to inspire creativity as well as function. Have fun with older kids and post cartoons or images of wardrobe "fails."

Play

Make it a game! When you are not rushing out the door, let your kids explore. Have a bin full of gear and morph into a meteorologist. Create an accent, find a prop, improvise a microphone (have fun!), make a weather forecast and have your children quickly dress for it. If they need other cues, flash a picture of the type of weather from an accessible book or magazine, or find an image on your phone, and have kids assemble the proper outfit. Increase the challenge appropriately for the age by using timers, teams or relay races. Incorporate into your morning routine. Take turns being the meteorologist, who checks the weather (simply step outside or use a media outlet) and reports back to the family on the forecast and clothing recommendations.

> To get out the door we sing "(Name) gets a coat, (Name) gets a coat, high ho the dairy-o, (Name) gets a coat. (Name) gets a zip...." for each of my three toddlers. Keeps everyone involved. ~ Tina F.

Trial & Error

All of us want to be in charge, so involve kids in the preparation for an outing. Have outerwear accessible and let them experiment. Give them the "reins" when not embarking on an extended excursion, and the consequences of experimentation are low. Help your child reflect on what worked and what didn't. Ask, "Did you bring enough clothing? Did you have the right layers? What would you do differently next time?"

After lots of trial and error, my son has discovered exactly what he needs when he goes outside to dig in the garden or climb his favorite cherry tree: his hat, puffy jacket, and boots. Pants? He's concluded they're superfluous.

Set the Tone

Ruth Ann Schabacker reminds us, "Each day comes, bearing its own gifts." In that vein proclaim, "What a beautiful day!" and mean it every day. Find the joy in each season and each kind of weather. Identify the different sensations to improve attitudes and elicit excitement: "The rain tickles my nose!"; "Hey! The snow is making a nice blanket for the animals."; "Ooh. It smells like fall." Adopting this simple habit worked wonders for me when I first moved to Oregon, a tired mom with a newborn and two-year old. As the ones who set the tone for our kids, we can help them embrace the day - only if we do it first.

Other Helpful Items

- warm, waterproof footwear
- full raingear
- reusable handwarmers
- sunscreen & sun hat
- extra hats & gloves
- binoculars & field guides
- field journal with pencils, erasers & glue stick in a small pouch
- collection pouch (for special found items)
- camera that kids can use
- glow sticks (at night)

Essential Gear

Do you have an essential piece of gear?

Each member of our family has an accessible bin of their outerwear/gear. They can choose what they need, which develops independence and avoids power struggles. ~ Nancy M.

Backpacks for everyone, no matter how small. Helps build their sense of responsibility and self-reliance. ~ Mike K.

I'm a huge fan of full rain gear, abeko type overalls for kids as outer pants, insulated boots, one-piece suits for littles, anything that helps us be warm, so we can really stay out for hours. ~ Kaye J.

We often pack plastic eggs with treats and take turns hiding them along the trail so that others can find them. ~ Lisa L.

First-aid kit. Kids can have their own and in non-urgent situations, can explore the best strategy to address an injury. ~ Dahvi W.

Stormy, our dog. ~ Ruth B.

I carry a bigger pack than necessary with extra gear and to stuff clothes into as they are being shed throughout the day. Kevin T.

Mom - she is the essential piece in the equation - she rocks. Other than that water and a snack is always helpful when things inevidably take longer than planned. ~ John R.

How Does Nature Spell Your Name?

Find letters, names and words in natural objects

As a kid I fell in love with a photographer who found letters and numbers in butterfly wings. I extended this game inside finding faces in knotty pine walls or names in scrolly, vine wallpaper. I was also the kid who, between riding and hiking adventures, spent countless hours watching shape-shifting clouds, flames licking the black night, or waves lapping the shore. We all become mesmerized by this primitive T.V. and the longer we look, the more we see, the greater our awareness for changes and patterns, cycles and processes. These scavenger hunts provide constant engagement in or out of the house, establish deep connections to the world, and build observation and inquiry skills.

Other Items to Find

- The alphabet, numbers or inspirational words and phrases
- Names of family, friends or pets
- Words to describe the day, the place or geologic features
- Vocabulary words or terms that pertain to the area

Explore

What "scavenger hunts" captivate your family? Look for the letters of names within natural materials. Record them in journals, with a phone or camera. Challenge older children with different words or vocabulary. For example, find the word "lichen" in a patch of lichen. What other names can be spelled? What other words can be found? Try to find all letters of a word in just oak tree branches, just fungi, cracks in stone paths or spider webs.

Discover

What kinds of materials make the best "As" or the best "Os"? Why? Will the letters withstand a rainstorm or a hot day? Will other letters appear in different seasons? The challenge of identifying change in a place connects us with that place. Apply this approach on the trail, on regular errand routes around town or at any place you visit frequently. Your crew will be too busy to "ugh" or drag their feet, and each visit to the same site will be fresh and new.

Extend

Before going to a new site, predict: What kind of materials will you find? Where would be the best place to look for particular letters? Bring others into the game; siblings and/or friends can choose the words and challenge each other. Create a scavenger hunt or use the general concept to create your own game.

Share

Share drawings and/or photographs of your letters and words with family and friends. Assemble them in a collection titled, "How Does Nature Spell?" On subsequent outdoor adventures, continue to look for your name, but also find someone else's name or other inspirational words. How happy would grandma be if she received a sign, expressing "I love you" or "Happy Birthday" in this natural, thoughtful and creative way?

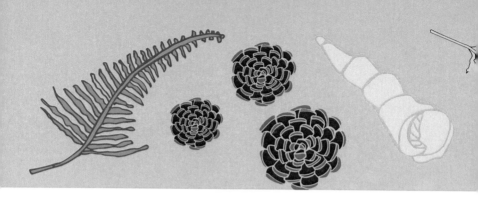

Amble On

Tap into the imagination to get everyone exploring

When my daughter was two, she was smitten with ballet. **On one trip we found the smooth spiral insides of wavy turban shells strewn all over the beach. As kids do she began to collect the shells, and we moved for hours up and down the beach collecting them. When I inquired further she declared, "They're ballerinas." On that trip her pile of ballerinas performed on sandy stages, twirled across our breakfast table and one came home to our bathtub where she dances the** *Nutcracker* **at bath time. Over time, I learned that I could engage this creative inspiration whenever we visited other beaches, hiked trails or just needed to move along! We collect feathers and tuck them into her hair and into the legs of her tights. She becomes Odille while I hum music from** *Swan Lake*, **and she jeté's down the path.**

Explore
Our children's imagination and interests are an instant hook we can use to help them engage and explore their world. What captures your child's imagination right now? Is it trains? Fairies? Airplanes? Dogs? Maybe it's a character from a book, TV show or movie.

By capitalizing on interests that already exist we can help them explore natural materials, encourage their creativity and possibly (hopefully!) move down the trail, path or sidewalk!

Play Set the stage at the beginning of a hike by enthusiastically suggesting, "We're going to build an airplane today!" Alternately, you can challenge the group, "Do you think we can build a cat on this hike?" or "How might we build a train?" As we wander I encourage my group of train-lovers, for example, to look for items that resemble train cars. In order to minimize impact, one guideline is to only collect items on the ground or only harvest one or two leaves off a living tree. Along the way we pick up pine cones, interesting rocks, pieces of bark, driftwood, seed pods or nuts, we find on the ground. This keeps kids on the move as they scurry down the trail to collect interesting bits. When we stop for lunch or a break, we begin to assemble our train. We make a train station, draw tracks in the dirt, create piles of items to transport - the possibilities are endless!

Extend While building examine the materials and ask questions to prompt curiosity: Who lived in this shell? Why is this stone so soft? Who's been eating these nuts or seeds? What created these lines on this stick. Likewise, explore a range of building styles and discuss different techniques: how to keep a roof from falling down; or how to attach one train car to the next; or why use rails instead of roads? Walking back to the car, tell a story about the train. The group can add details too! The story will help carry tired kids back to the trailhead.

Draw a map of the adventure, mark special stops along the trail, and let the kids help you decide what you will do at those special spots. Examples: read another chapter from a beloved book, eat a special snack, play a game, sketch something cool we have found, or, a recent favorite, paint one toenail! ~ Laura H.

Fox Walking

Many outdoor schools teach Fox Walking–a way of moving along a trail or through a natural area, making as little sound as possible. To begin remind everyone that a fox only eats if it can sneak up on its prey and to do that it must be very, very quiet. After folks calm their bodies, prick their ears, bend their knees and lift their noses to smell the air, they begin moving down the trail. Instead of tromping and using a heavy heel strike, walk on the balls of feet and lower the center of gravity. With each step test the ground with a "snooping toe" to make sure no sound is made by stepping on dry leaves or twigs. These snaps and rustles alert prey. In this way explore what surfaces muffle steps and which give foxes away. Don't be surprised when "foxes" begin sneaking up on each other or practice approaching wildlife without being detected. You will find that the magic of Fox Walking will quiet even the loudest, most boisterous child.

A Guide for the Guide

Fox Walking and so many other games and nature-based activities are described by the Wilderness Awareness School in Duvall, Washington. They can be adapted to any environment, any number of kids and any age group. If you find yourself or your kids wanting more of these types of activities, check out the "Animal Forms" section of *Coyote's Guide to Connecting with Nature* by Jon Young, Ellen Haas and Ewan McGown. This outdoor educator's tome has greatly informed the Let the Kid Guide approach and provides us endless inspiration.

Trail Movers

What helps your child move down the trail?

We like to have multiple modes of toddler transport - walking, backpack, shoulders, swinging between our hands - keeps the forward momentum! ~ Kate. G.

A hiking stick is a huge motivator. ~ Betsy T.

Taking time to stop, inspect and talk about whatever they feel is interesting. It always works to keep them motivated. ~ Ben W.

We take turns hiding gummy bunnies along the trail, a treat we only have on adventures. ~ Andy A.

"Let's race to that tree." "Hurry! Hide behind that bush so we can jump out at Dada!" "Uh oh, I think I hear a T-Rex coming. Ruuuuuuuuuun!" ~ Renee R.

Trying to keep up with the dogs and telling stories from when I was a kid walking the same trails. ~ Will S.

We have an only child. Another kid helps a lot! ~ Amy T.

Working up to a challenge: We did not do our favorite bike ride the whole way the first time. We explored further and further each time, and then one day were able to ride all the way. ~ Lisa R.

Curiosity. What's coming up next?! ~ Tessa L.

Live Like an Animal

Animal play: A pathway to knowledge, compassion and understanding

Some days it's like living in a menagerie. **Humpback whale whistles, clicks, and grunts, jolting my husband and me out of our pre-dawn slumber. A little drowsy, and very hungry, he demands krill for breakfast. We roll out of bed and meet farm cat in the kitchen: "How did you sleep, Honey?" "Mao." "Would you like some breakfast?" "Mao." I turn back to find my whale with socks on his hands and an apple in his mouth. "Are those your flippers, Whale?" Leaning forward to drop the apple onto the table he declares, "No, Mama Owl. These are my wings..." and continues to explain the mouse he caught in his talons for breakfast. "Thank you, Great Horned Owl," I quickly switch gears, trying to keep up. That exchange summons shrieks from the other side of the kitchen table; getting back on my game (before tea has been poured!) I respond, "Would you like a mouse too, Sister Screech Owl?"**

Play Children naturally mimic animals. Use the animals that are important to you and your kids to play games. Modify your favorites: "Redlight-Greenlight" becomes a predator-prey game; change Blob Tag to Pack or Herd Tag, emphasizing teamwork and communication. Challenge the group to come up with their own variations. Also, try some yoga; it brims with animal-inspired poses: downward dog, dolphin, cat-cow, crow. Ever play "Bear-Mosquito-Fish"? Divide a big group in half and teach a body movement for each animal. Teams secretly decide what animal to be and line-up facing each other along a center line. When animals are revealed, bear chases fish, who chases mosquito, who chases bear. Tag "animals" to join your group before they reach a predetermined safety zone.

Extend

Animals are teachers who offer valuable lessons. By imitating animals we not only improve our physical abilities and our understanding of them, but, perhaps even more significant, mental attitudes can be learned. As my family watches squirrels relentlessly harvest hickory nuts in the fall, we discuss the importance of hard work and focus on a critical task for winter survival. Maybe it's the patience and precision of a great blue heron stalking a fish or the long-range vision of a raptor that speaks to us. A dog wagging its tail spreads smiles across our faces, reminding us how our body language and attitude are contagious; without saying a word, we have the opportunity to impact those around us profoundly. Encourage your children to identify other lessons from animals they observe. Along with pictures drawn or photographs printed of the animals, label not only unique body parts and adaptations, but also add notes on behavior, natural history and lessons learned.

Storytime: Let quieter voices be heard

Who doesn't love storytelling? Whether alone with your child or in a group start an "And Then" story about a favorite animal. The first person begins the story. The next person adds another sentence beginning with "and" or "and then." For example:

Once upon a time there was a beaver who lived in a pond. AND the beaver lived with it's mother, father and three sisters AND they lived in a lodge made of mud and sticks AND THEN one day the beaver heard an alarming "crack" in the forest AND THEN...."

Each person adds what they know about that particular animal. This game also helps us practice listening and cooperation skills. An added bonus is quieter kids get drawn into the conversation and all have a good laugh when inevitably the story goes rogue.

Expand

It's sometimes difficult to urge our kids out of the role of a particular animal. Expand their experience with this animal by identifying the other animals with which it interacts: who does it compete with for food or shelter? Who does it prey on? If a prey animal, who preys on it? In a totally different landscape, in which the favorite animal does not exist, what animal fills its role in the new community?

> As the day begins review what challenges your child might face: a soccer match, a group project or public speaking: "I need the speed of a wolf today, the patience to work in a pack and a clear, strong howl, so my voice and ideas are heard."

Discover

Back at home learn as much as you can about your favorite animals through books, videos and observations. Identify characteristic body parts and behavior, habitat and food preferences, or foraging strategies. Collect as much information about the animal as possible. In your backyard or when visiting any site, survey the area and ask: If you were that animal, where would you live? Where would you gather food? What would your food sources be in each environment? What dangers could be around each corner?

Share

Develop the stories of all the animals in this web through imaginative play, storytelling and artwork. Create your own animal guide book, organized by type of animal (Example: mammals, reptiles, birds) or habitat (Example: woods, fields, waterways). For each page include a picture, label its unique parts and list some of its behaviors. Also include any special stories or experiences with the animal, poems, songs or books about the animal. If you've created a game using the animal, add the instructions and a diagram to your guide. Continue to add to it. Proudly display it with other books or field guides in the house and share it with family and friends.

Kid's Eye View

Capitalize on our fascination with screens when outside

A few weeks after a trip to the beach, I sorted the photos on our family camera and discovered a series I didn't recognize. At first, all I noticed was the difference in perspective. There were many close-ups, photos looking upwards and shots of the backs of our heads as we drove. The next photo revealed the photographer: my three-year-old, camera to her eye, snapping a picture of herself in the side mirror of our van. She inspects her surroundings on film and experiments with her reflection. Many of the photos were out of focus; two of her stuffed mouse; three of her feet, but this surprise "selfie" is one of my favorite pictures from that time in her life. It's framed and displayed prominently in our house, showing her that we value her creativity.

Explore Let your child wander like a dog and take pictures of whatever they choose. Resist the urge to edit, guide and control. Spend time along a trail, explore the beach, yard or local park, and meander at their pace. Empower the activity by joining in with your own camera. Alternatively, encourage your child to focus on one a subject: heart-shaped rocks, cloud shapes, sticks that look like critters, organisms in a tide pool or dogs met along the trail. Take photos of these subjects to create a collection.

Discover

At home play with adding filters, cropping, and editing the photos. Smartphones these days have a large array of editing options that are intuitive and accessible. Print favorites, create a collage, assemble in a small album or frame them. Explore different apps. We found one that allows your child to create and narrate a story using their own photographs and words. Powerful.

Share

Shooting, printing, displaying and gifting projects from children's photographs promotes the value of creative work and validates their creative choices and expression. In your home create a gallery: use painter's tape to safely hang art on walls; or erect a line and, with clothespins, have your child hang up their work. Invite family and friends to a gallery walk. Can't join in person? No problem! Grab a phone!

Extend

Simple video editing software is accessible, easy to use and standard on most computers. Allow your child to film highlights of an outing. Splice photographs and videos together with sound effects, music and a variety of transitions. Help them cut and string the clips together to proudly share their adventure.

> Giving Lou a camera has changed her view of hikes. We may not get too far, but she is examining every nook and cranny with the camera and loves to go through the photos. ~ Betsy T.

Helpful Apps for the Field

Apps change, but here are a few we use with our kids right now.

- Merlin Bird ID for bird identification
- Leaf Snap to help identify plants
- Sky Guide gives a full view of the night sky where you live
- Audubon Guides are available digitally and easily downloaded onto phones

Invisibility Cloak

Use camouflage to observe and merge with natural surroundings

In the summer months I lead kids' adventure camps in Oregon. On the first day of camp, we head out to a field of tall grasses, blackberry mounds and snowberry bushes, to play a hide and seek game called Eagle Eye. I inevitably hear some hemming and hawing from the kids about prickers, ticks, not wanting to get dirty–the usual excuses. What I find: soon after the first game, the kids learn to tuck deeply into the brush and get nose-to-nose with spiders or lay flat on the ground in the tall grasses where they closely examine an ant trail. Often kids are detected because they just can't bear to let the ripe clumps of blackberries go unpicked while they hide next to them. At the end of the week the kids are begging to play Eagle Eye at every site we visit. They learn to come to camp in clothes that will blend into the forest and learn to sit still, wait and watch–magic.

Play Find a forested patch of land or shrubby area. This could be in a park, a local forest or grassland or maybe even a backyard. Look around and ask your child what the plants look like. Are they green and bushy? Brown and dry? Grassy and open? Shaded or light-filled? Camouflage skin with dirt or mud. Alternatively, collect plant materials off the ground, like leafy branches, grass seed heads, sticks or moss. Now the fun begins! Decorate hair and clothes with it. Use twine or yarn to help connect pieces together. Can you weave some branches into a "hat" to cover hair? Can you dangle thin branches over shoulders or hold leafy branches to create a disguise? Participate with your child. It's always more fun when grown-ups play too!

Discover

With your child's new camouflage, find a spot where they can sit and hide for a few minutes; lengthen the time each time they hide. Ask them what they notice. Do the birds sound different? Did they see any critters? What do they smell? With young children you can hide with them: snuggle-up together, watch, observe and be still. When we are camouflaged, we become part of the landscape, not the center of it. This perspective change can be a profound shift in the way we experience the world, and the way we conduct ourselves within it.

Field Note

Camouflage is one adaptation that many organisms use to blend into their surroundings. Using a few tricks, we can camouflage ourselves to see wildlife and other mysteries. If we drop inhibitions and immerse into this activity, we will discover many surprises about the world and even, perhaps, about ourselves.

Extend

With this new-found knowledge, play classic games, like Hide & Seek, Thicket, Sardines or Eagle Eye. Improved "invisibility" skills will make you tough to beat. Don't have enough people for a game? Test your invisibility with other critters. Can you enter their world unnoticed? Find a spot, be still and see what emerges.

Sit Spot

Many naturalists and primitive arts practitioners like Tom Brown, Jr. and Jon Young, advocate visiting a special outside sit spot every day to get to know it intimately. Visit your spot in the rain, snow, throughout the seasons and learn what creatures live or pass through there. Pay attention to what you hear, smell, see, feel and possibly taste at your spot. Note the smell of wet rotting leaves or blackberries warming in the sun. Hear the alarm call of a squirrel as you approach and what happens in the forest after the cry of a red tail hawk. With young children go together to your spot. Encourage young ones to sit quietly and observe. As you sit cloaked in silence and stillness, you can blend into the landscape and find that many secrets once invisible to you, are slowly revealed.

Fuel to Fill Empty Tanks

What foods are key on an adventure?

Power Food Cheese, jerky, salami or summer sausage, PB&J, GORP (Good Old Raisins & Peanuts), avocado, hummus, frozen go-gurts

Fruit 'n Veggies Apples, grapes, dried fruit, easy-to-peel oranges, fruit or veggie pouches, carrots, sugar snap peas

Other Popcorn, crackers, goldfish, graham crackers, gummies, pretzels, a treat they don't usually get (or only get on an adventure).

Drinks Water is the best option and should be consumed the most; a few other special beverages for the trail include peppermint tea, hot chocolate, and juices low in sugar and watered down.

Power Pellets

Want to really power-up for an adventure? Make your own energy nuggets. You can find many recipes online. This one has been refined by our good friend and fellow "guide," Laura.

1 cup oatmeal
1/2 cup peanut butter
1/3 cup honey
1 tsp vanilla

2/3 cup coconut
1/2 cup ground flax seed
1 Tbsp chia seeds
Fun options: chocolate, craisins, spirulina

Mix all ingredients together, chill in the refrigerator for an hour, then form into balls. Store in fridge or freezer. Enjoy!

Map My World

Root down to create positive impact in your place

As a child, I knew my backyard better than my best friend.
I knew the best climbing trees, the best place to find potato
bugs, the best places to hide, the places to avoid poison ivy and
yellow jackets, where to find my cat in a rainstorm, where the
red-shouldered hawk perched, where to run barefoot and where
not to (under the chestnut trees, of course!). Children naturally
create intricate and intimate internal maps of their immediate
surroundings. These maps create a foundation for exploration,
self-reliance, discovery and confidence. It is a reference point
from which they draw throughout their lives. Help build this foundation and reinforce their innate desire to survey their place.

Wendell Berry
famously said,
"If you don't
know where
you are, you
don't know
who you are."

Connect

Find a place to sit outside. Maybe it's a hammock
or blanket in the grass, a chair on the porch or
balcony. Maybe it's in a favorite tree, at a neighborhood park or at Grandpa's house. Slow down.
Sit and observe what you see, hear, smell and feel.
To help "tune-in" make two lists: "Day of" and
"Season of" observations. This simple act will
cultivate presence, pique awareness and usher in
discoveries over time.

Play Begin by helping your child create a 3D model of your place using blocks, sticks, pinecones and miniature figures. Allow your child to manipulate objects in the model by adding the details that are important to them. Alternatively, you can use a large piece of paper and help your child create a map of the area. Mark the location and orientation of the structures, like your house and driveway, any outbuildings, location of trees, garden, bird feeders, sandbox, sidewalk, fire hydrant, fences and bird nests. Use a compass to mark directions on the map. Help your child label each item on the map and create a key.

Encourage your child to identify trees and plants that live in your yard. At first stick to the big picture: shrubs, flowering plants, trees that lose leaves in the winter versus trees that keep leaves. What mammals live in the trees? What birds come to your feeders. How many pairs of mourning doves visit? Do neighboring pets come to explore? Where do you find ladybugs, lizards and worms? Where do you smell lilacs or honeysuckle? In the morning or evening, listen and identify birds with the help of Merlin Bird ID app from Cornell's Lab of Ornithology. Use the Smithsonian's LeafSnap app to identify plants. When ready follow your family's interests to go deeper with a topic.

Discover

> To broaden our perspective of the world, we build a map of our living room with blocks. One of us hides a favorite stuffed animal in the living room and then marks on the block map where the treasure was hidden, challenging the others to find it. The children love to take turns re-hiding the treasure and marking the "x" on the block map. This is great practice for map reading on the trail. ~ Kevin H.

Expand

Does the map change with the seasons? What changes when it's raining? Are there any nighttime elements to add? What other special spots exist? Can you find a roost for bats, a mosquito zone, a shadow tag play area? Now, think about the life in your yard. How do our choices impact the critter community? How do they influence us? Profound learning comes from understanding our place and our role in it. This discovery process increases our empathy for the species around us and elicits reflection about how we choose to live in the world.

> It's the little things citizens do.
> That's what will make the difference.
> My little thing is planting trees.
>
> ~ Wangari Maathai
> Nobel Peace Prize Recipient

Community Impact

Connecting to our place and its creatures compels us to play an active role in it. How? A leader in place-based education, Teton Science Schools uses design thinking to examine a place and ultimately make a positive impact. First, notice what you already do to better your place. Do you: grow native plants or flowers that attract pollinators; use reusable bags for snack; beautify your sidewalk with chalk art; donate books, toys and clothes? Are there more opportunities to make an impact? Ask community members for ideas and consider all aspects - ecology, culture and economy - of your place. Defining a need provides an opportunity to create a solution. Generate multiple ideas and evaluate which is the best that is feasible for you at this time. Then go for it! Sometimes these projects are challenging, but the sense of satisfaction and benefit to your community reward your hard work.

Active Citizen One industrious 6th-grader, in the Place Network of the Teton Science Schools, noticed construction waste in his neighborhood and repurposed discarded 2x4s into building blocks. He reduced landfill waste, developed wood-working skills and donated a high-quality toy to a local daycare. Outstanding.

Music of the Night

Build comfort and confidence in the dark

It was a perfect autumn evening: the light glowed off the changing tree leaves, and my toddlers happily played in the yard, digging in the raised bed outside the kitchen window. I prepared dinner in peace, occasionally glancing out the window at their play, able to enjoy and actually retain the story broadcasted on the radio. Our slamming screen door shattered the magic, my son hysterically shouting, "Mama! Mama! The sun went down!" Although he never before was afraid of the dark, watching the sun disappear below the horizon impacted him deeply. There are many things that are unsettling when day becomes night, and it manifests in different ways. Our challenge is to help our children find comfort in the night. In doing so they will gain confidence and be empowered when faced with mystery and darkness at other times in their lives.

Comfort

How do you get comfortable? Like the animals, make a nest or a burrow, which provides protection from the elements, as well as protection from predators. What would a squirrel do? What would an owl and its owlets do? Pile on warm clothes. Bring a favorite animal, blanket or a sleeping bag. Use a camp chair or sleeping pad, to avoid losing heat sitting directly on the ground. Snuggle in a hammock or porch swing. Find a place to sit that is familiar in the day. Playing I Spy, identify the elements of that place with the little light available and some logic; even if not seen, what do we know is there? As you practice, getting comfortable in the dark will take less and less time.

Connect

Build your stillness stamina. Sit quietly—back-to-back, solo, in laps, or whatever is appropriate for your child—for a set amount of time. With hands cupped behind your ears, put on your "deer ears," to amplify sound and quiet your bodies. Begin with silence for however long your child can stand it. Every time you go out, try to push that time a little further. Record your time and challenge that time for the next night out. Little do they know these games are expanding comfort levels in the dark. And once comfortable, there is no dearth of nighttime activities to explore.

Night Games Safety

Before kids are unleashed into the dark, identify a few parameters for safety. Have everyone brainstorm and agree on some ground rules before the fun begins. For example:

- Set clear boundaries for where the kids are allowed to play and a point past which they should not venture.

- Ensure games take place well away from busy roads. Ask kids to regularly check that everyone is accounted for.

- Smaller kids should be buddied up with an older child, so that they are never wandering around on their own.

- Make a "gather-up" call to bring everyone out of hiding.

Remember: Playing in the dark is a great opportunity to expand the kids' comfort zones and their independence. You might be expanding yours too!

Discover

Now you are ready to illuminate the mysteries of the night. Play "I hear with my little ear," which provides opportunities to chat about nocturnal habits of animals, diurnal animals who are sleeping, non-living noises (like wind or water), as well as human-generated noises. Alternatively, while everyone sits quietly, indicate sounds heard by pointing in the sound's direction or squeezing hands. Raise eyebrows, look surprised, giggle softly at the sounds you hear.

> Understanding what's making the noises can help children temper the embrace the darkness and make more discoveries.

Explore

- **Dance party**: Search "moon songs" and make a playlist. (Examples: Moondance, Moonlight Sonata Dancing in the Moonlight, Fly Me to the Moon).

- **Compose your own midnight melodies**, using voices, simple percussion instruments and inspired by nighttime noises. Is there a consistent baseline: a flowing river or crashing waves? What is the main melody: spring peepers, crickets or katydids? Are there ephemeral qualities: dog barks, owl hoots or wind gusts?

- **Swing** on a swing-set as dusk turns dark.

- **Practice Fox Walking** (see page 22).

- **Sardines**: The reverse of hide-n-seek (i.e. one hides; all else seek) is even more fun in the dark.

- **Play Tag!** Try flashlight or moonshadow tag!

- **Plant a moon garden**. These blooms reflect the moonlight and attract night-time pollinators. There are many varieties: moonflower, evening primrose and night-blooming jasmine. Research which ones work best in your climate.

> **Obsidian I**
>
> It is the universal statement of a star, the message Orion has carried in winter through the ages:
>
> It is the dark which illuminates.
>
> ~ Lyn Dalebout

Get Cookin'

Campfire magnetism engages everyone in the preparation of a meal

I have fond memories of camping with my Girl Scout troop in northern Wisconsin. At dinner time we built a fire. While the coals developed we watched curiously as the Scout leader laid out ground meat, chopped onions, diced potatoes, canned corn and shredded cheese. She handed each of us a length of tinfoil and instructed us to fill it up. Each girl shuffled through the line, buffet style, rolled her ingredients into a pocket and placed it carefully in the coals of the fire. I vividly remember the magical moment, as I gingerly opened my pocket and a whiff of savory steam wafted out. I've been fascinated by cooking over a fire ever since.

Basics

Make sure that your fire is hot and has time to develop coals, approximately 30-60 minutes. While you wait to let the high flames die down, prepare your tools and food. Cooking on a stick and in tinfoil are two favorite campfire cooking styles. Look for green sticks that won't catch fire as easily as dry wood. Teach children to harvest from trees with lots of branches. Some campground trees are heavily harvested, so go for a walk to find a less impacted tree. Alternatively, use heavy aluminum foil or two sheets of regular foil. Cut foil into squares, fill with ingredients (recipes on the following pages) then fold the seams together to make a closed pouch. Place pouches in the coals or position a stick over the coals and wait. Not sure what to do now? A few ideas follow.

Explore

While you wait for the coals to develop or food to cook, take the opportunity to discuss any number of topics. How did early people cook their food? What type of vessels did they use? What skills would be essential in those times? How would you improvise cooking materials if you didn't have the modern tools you have today? Pretend you and your family are early settlers or explorers. As you prepare your meal, ask your children what they would eat if they had to survive off the land around them. These conversations can spur curiosity and problem solving as children contemplate challenges early people had in the collection and preparation of food.

Safety

Managing kids and fire can be tricky. Set up boundaries and fire safety guidelines that everyone follows. To gain buy-in, include the kids in the process.

Here are a few common sense precautions:

- Explore the elements of fire with kids. Fire is: hot, bright, warm, comforting, scary, etc.
- Have fire only when local laws allow and fire danger is low.
- Clear dry debris away from the fire circle to reduce the chance of fire jumping the ring.
- Keep water close by in case fire jumps the ring.
- Make fires in established fire circles.
- Make the fire area a walking zone.
- It's OK to play with sticks away from the fire but not near it.
- Always fully extinguish the fire before going to bed or leaving the campsite.

Develop your own rules to keep the kids and the landscape safe!

Bannock Bread

2 cups flour (can use half whole wheat)
1 Tbsp baking powder
1/2 tsp salt
2 Tbsp butter
1/2 cup warm water

Directions: In a bowl finger-mix all ingredients, except the water, until crumbly. Sprinkle a little water at a time, being careful not to add too much. It may seem that you don't have enough water, but keep working the dough until it holds together. It should be slightly more wet than biscuit dough.

Knead the dough so it stays together. (Add raisins for a sweeter treat!) Take a small handful and wrap it around the end of a green stick. Cook over coals for 10 - 12 minutes, rotating to cook evenly. Add a smear of butter, jam or honey. Delicious with any meal.

HINT: Mix the dry ingredients in a ziplock bag before going camping. Just add water to the bag and skip the bowl!

Banana Boats

Bananas (one per boat)
Chocolate chips, shredded coconut and/or chopped nuts

Directions: Cut a banana in 2 along the length (i.e. 2, crescent moons). Sprinkle chocolate chips and nuts over the flesh of the banana. Loosely wrap the banana in tinfoil and put it in the coals. Warm it for about 10 minutes. Turn carefully once during cooking. Enjoy!

The Big Picture

The importance of eating as a family is well documented. Fires have a magnetic draw that pulls us together. Sharing meals creates space for family connection and, when others are involved, building community. Meals are also key aspects of celebration. So mark a big adventure day, the learning of a new skill or just being together with a special fire-cooked meal.

Campfire Potatoes

Large baking potatoes
Thinly sliced whole onion (red or yellow)
Herb of choice: dill, parsley or thyme
Crumbled bacon or parmesan cheese

Directions: Slice potato widthwise almost all the way through, but leave enough to hold it together. Place onions between each potato slice. Sprinkle with crumbled bacon, parmesan and/or herbs. Wrap well with heavy aluminum foil and bury in the coals of the fire. Cooking time depends on potato size and fire strength. Rotate once or twice but leave basically untouched for ~45 minutes. Pierce with a fork; it should come out without lifitng the potato. Serve with butter and a few sprigs of parsley.

Cheese on a Stick

2" cubes of firm cheese like cheddar or monterey jack
Slices of baguette or bread
Garnishes: pickles, cured meat, olives, tomatoes or red pepper

Directions: Skewer one piece of cheese on the end of a stick. Roast slowly over the coals of your fire. Keep a close eye on it and keep the stick somewhat upright to avoid the cheese dropping into the fire. Once it starts getting soft, smear it on a piece of bread and serve with garnish.

In the Kitchen!

These recipes are just a starting point to inspire your family. When we include children in the process we increase their buy-in and engagement, around the campfire and also in the kitchen. They will think of other ingredients or invent an entirely new meal. Support their ideas. It may not sound good to you, but let them make their own choices, discoveries and mistakes. Who knows? Your family may really like peanut butter-macaroni-n-cheese-pickle pockets!

Connect the Drops

Delightful ideas for rainy days

Few things excite me more on a rainy-day adventure than finding worm trails in the dirt road that runs through the pear orchards behind our 1905 farmhouse. One winter our family spent many hours finding, observing and tracking those trails. Where do they go? Why does this one divert left? What surface lays the foundation for the best trails? Why does this trail disappear? A big worm must have made this one! And finally the reward of finding the worm making the trail, followed by subsequent shrieks of surprise and excitement (from the kids too!) as we track our friend. One of the many gifts of rain. Without it we would have little opportunity to delight in worm trails.

Recall Let's face it. Most of us "ugh" when it rains. We want to curl up, slurp savory soup and stay inside. But do you remember a time when that wasn't the case? When we'd find the biggest puddles to stomp, stand under a gutter-fall or shake a branch and watch the drops splatter an unsuspecting sibling? Remember when we'd do everything to avoid a rainstorm, but when caught, absolutely delight in it? Let the following ideas remind you of the fun you had in the rain as a kid and try them with your kids.

> "When you see someone putting on his Big Boots,
> you can be pretty sure an Adventure is going to happen."
>
> ~ A.A.Milne, *Winnie the Pooh*

Mindset

As adults we place hurdles in our path that prevent us from embracing the rain: "It's cold; it's wet; we'll get dirty," are a few. How can we capture the chld-like exuberance and freedom of playing in the rain? This playful mindset is key to forgetting the cold, wet and mud, so we can focus on rainy day fun.

What is your favorite memory from playing in the rain?
Connect to these memories, and you'll be able to enjoy the drops.

- **During a warm, summer deluge don swimsuits,** armed with washable markers, draw silly faces, words and tattoos on yourself, or even more fun, on each other.

- **Don't have boots?** Design your own with duct tape and plastic bags. Each with a unique prototype, test designs in various trials. Enhance the ensemble with a garbage bag slicker.

- **Puddle-stomping contest**: Shoot for the biggest splash or most style. Play follow the leader and bound through ephemeral gutter-streams, wet bushes and drips. Create an obstacle course or relay race. Winners? Those who are the goofiest, actively participating and laughing the most.

- **Where do the animals go?** How do they stay warm and dry? Go on a safari to find animals, domestic or wild. Or find a hideout for yourself. Bring a thermos of soup to your shelter and "camp out" for awhile.

- **Create a unique rhythm or melody:** Set out containers of various materials, sizes and shapes and note the sounds. Make some music!

- **Abstract art:** Drip food coloring or powdered tempera paint on heavy stock paper during a light rain. When some rain has collected, tip the page and let the paint streak down, around, from side-to-side. Experiment with this technique and see what emerges. Bring artwork inside to dry.

- **"Singing in the Rain:"** Create and film your own skit!

Create

While warming up and sipping tea or hot cocoa, talk about what appeared on your canvas, what you found following flowing water or other deluge discoveries. Make a collection of rainy day artwork or short stories. Fold a few pieces of white paper and a piece of construction paper in half, staple down the middle and decorate the construction paper cover. Perhaps the artwork highlights favorite things about rainy days or a book about the gifts of rain, such as flowers, puddles and bigger waterfalls. Use these kid-generated books to change droopy attitudes and remind us of the playful potential of these days. With these books, reconnect with your rollicking, rainy-day self and celebrate the rain!

Songs

We all know "Singing in the Rain," "Itsy Bitsy Spider" and perhaps, "If All the Raindrops Were Gumdrops and Lemondrops." Personalize these songs with your own additions. Pick an aspect to change: instead of "singing" what other actions can you be doing in the rain? Sing and play follow the leader inspired by your new lyrics. Additionally, replace "spider" with another animal or take turns choosing two favorite foods and have everyone sing along to their new song. This is great to sing while putting on rain gear and even better to sing outside in the rain. Enjoy this chance to be silly and creative with your kids.

> Around us, life bursts with miracles,
> a glass of water, a ray of sunshine, a leaf,
> a caterpillar, a flower, laughter, raindrops.
>
> ~ Thich Nhat Hanh
> Zen Master, Peace Activist

Extend

Follow the water! Float a "boat" of any kind down a rivulet, gutter or other stream created by the rain. See how far you can follow it. Where does the water go? Does it eventually flow into a treatment plant? If it goes straight into a river or stream, what does that do to it? Consider making signs to share where the water goes. Not only is it fun to follow water, we can improve our understanding of how everything is connected and our impact on our place.

It Takes a Village

How do you involve siblings and friends to help each other?

I catch myself saying, "This family doesn't work unless we're all helping," something my mom told us all the time growing up. ~ Ginger R.

My older daughter loves to hold her younger sister's hand as they cross the street or walk down the trail. She also likes to teach her safety tips, which is great reinforcement for herself. ~ Katelynn R.

We role play different characters in stories as we hike along. Each member of the family is an animal who helps each other to solve a problem. ~ Nancy B.

I like to promote the idea of being a "team" rather than racing or trying to beat one another. ~ Kyla L.

When one child falls or is having a tough time with a hike or bike ride, we encourage the other child(ren) to check in with the one that's struggling. They then offer support, a bite of a special snack or a pat on the back. ~ Kristen K.

I give positive feedback when my kids help each other. ~ Annie S.

Taking turns finding something of a certain color. Taking turns as the leader. Taking turns is key. ~ Kendra W.

Kids by nature want to help. Let them look around and observe who needs help and then let them initiate how. You'll see them blossom and you'll see the other child light up also. ~ Mike P.

Snow Dome

A winter shelter invites teamwork & playfulness

A few winters ago we had a huge storm. It hit at night and left us with two feet of snow. In the morning, my three-year-old daughter awoke with squeals of delight. A dawdler by nature, she wolfed down her breakfast, dressed herself and ran out into the snow. Her father plowed the driveway, leaving a large pile next to the ponderosa pine tree in the front yard. Mom, Dad, Nana and Poppy all joined her digging, building, creating her first snow fort. After we finished, her stuffed mouse joined us in the hollowed-out pile of snow, snuggling together. Years later, she still talks about that experience. Every time it snows, she runs outside to the pine tree and asks us to join her in building a fort. The excitement and wonder in her face when she peers outside and sees the snow falling is reminiscent of my own childhood and taps into a deeper well of joy and playfulness that still lives inside me. With children in our lives, snow days are exuberant, creative opportunities for everyone in the family to be playful.

Snow Safety

- Never dig or play in a snow cave alone or near a road where plows may operate.
- Never crawl on top of a dome.
- Maintain ventilation inside the dome.

Emphasize the communal aspect of building: Leading vs. following, grunt work vs. skilled work, digging snow vs. removing snow. Feel the satisfaction and reward of working together as a team.

Nuts & Bolts

1. Survey the area. What structures exist in the landscape that will help the fort? Is there a snow bank, a snow-covered bush or a tree well, for a useful starting point? Then build a large pile of snow. Think about the mound's size and shape, which will determine the fort's.

2. Send everyone to collect 12" long twigs. Get a few handfuls each. Make sure the sticks are about the same length. These will be the thickness of the walls and roof.

3. Poke sticks into the snow all over the mound. Make sure they go in all the way. Then pack down the snow using hands and bodies. Be careful to pack evenly and look out for getting poked with sticks.

4. Take a break. If you can bear to wait, two or more hours is best to allow the snow to set up.

5. Pick a spot for your door and start digging. As you hollow out the inside of your fort, look for the tips of your sticks. These are the markers that indicate when to stop digging in that direction. The uniform length of the sticks will keep the walls even and strong.

6. Let it flow. Create a ventilation hole in the roof of your dome.

7. Celebrate! Nice work, Team! Now let's have more snow-fun together!

Stay Warm!

When the thermometer hangs around freezing, we need a solid strategy for outside play. Children lose heat much faster than adults, so it's critical to choose the right clothing to keep kids warm and happy. While fancy outdoor clothing is effective, it's not necessary to spend their college savings on it. Think "wick, warm, weather" from page 14. For warm layers use materials other than cotton. Wool is warm even when wet; so are inexpensive poly-blends, like those colorful fleeces found at secondhand stores. A raincoat over a warm fleece is a practical system on a snowy day.

Play

Now it's time for fun! Have snacks and pretend it's seal meat or dried berries collected from summer. Have a snow dome celebration and bring blankets and hot cocoa inside. Create a snow cake and decorate it with seeds, nuts and bits of vegetables that you can leave out for critters to find and eat. Fill bowls with fresh snow and drizzle with maple syrup. Make believe you are a bear family or squirrel family. What do these animals do to take shelter and keep warm? How do they play?

Extend

Build forts in other seasons and habitats, using different materials. Notice how available materials in that place define the type of shelter that can be made. How does stone, clay, straw or sticks inform the structure's design? Search online for "debris huts" and try them out. As you experiment, you will understand why certain design choices were made and how form follows function.

Helpful Hints

Do your best with the gear you have. No snow boots? A thick pair of wool socks under rain boots works. Be sure they aren't too tight; decreased circulation prevents blood from warming extremities. Wool or poly-blend socks are crucial in the cold - absolutely no cotton socks on a snow day! Mittens that fit well (try the zip-up kind), help decrease frustration and improve attitudes. Slip a hand in boots or mittens to check little ones' fingers and toes often. If kids are getting chilled that's always a good time to stop for hot cocoa!

Let It Snow

What are other ways to enjoy the snow?

We don't always have the time (or enough snow!) to build forts and domes. What else can we do? Whether it's the first snow of the season or the twentieth storm, beat the cold. With these starter ideas, head out and embrace winter.

Playful

The usual snow games are timeless for a reason. Build snowmen, make snow angels, romp around, ambush each other with snow balls, shake tree branches for unexpected snow showers or play an epic game of hide-and-seek and try not to leave tracks!

Tune-in

After a new snowfall, head outside to see who's been walking through your yard or neighborhood. Find a set of tracks to follow. Which direction are they going? What are they doing? What other signs do you notice? What's the story they tell?

Celebrate

Inevitably your crew will want to eat the snow. Find a clean batch and make snow treats. Try snow cones with maple syrup and cinnamon or snow cream with sweetened condensed milk. Make a snow cake for neighborhood critters. Decorate the area with snow sculptures and natural materials. If it's almost Winter Solstice, bear witness and revel in the lengthening daylight.

Purpose increases snow play stamina. Some of us are motivated by tasks: snow and ice removal or lightening the snow load on bushes and trees (perhaps onto your brother!). Add a dog into the equation? Kids stay out more. Another kid? Likewise. On the subject of animals, why not try to find some? Follow tracks; look for signs. What happens to critters on snowy days? What would you do? I know what my daughter would do: puffed up like a marshmallow in all her layers, plop into a pile of snow and feast on the fluffy, white treat. What else increases snow play stamina? You joining the fun!

Outside In
Indoor activities that build the budding naturalist

The fragrance of paperwhites reminds me of the holidays of my childhood, so in preparation for my parent's arrival one Thanksgiving, we forced some bulbs. My kids were eager for NaNa and Moose's arrival; however they were still developing the ability to understand time, and three weeks meant nothing to them. With calendar in hand I stated, "They will be here on this day, about when the bulbs bloom." We drew little pots with bulbs on the calendar and decided every week to draw the sprouts and measure their height. A couple of weeks into the project, my son woke me at 5:30AM, ruler in hand, emphatic, "Mama, it's time to measure the bulbs."

Teachable Moments

What started as a task to create holiday cheer, developed into an opportunity not only to "count down" the arrival of grandparents and Thanksgiving, but also to observe the growth of paperwhites over time.

Many of us find ourselves in the midst of these happy accidents. The key is to grab the teachable moment to go deeper with your kids. Often this occurs by bringing the outside in.

How-To Force Paperwhites

1. Fill a tall, glass container (no drainage holes) with two inches of pebbles that have been rinsed of dust.

2. Add 1-2 Tbsp of aquarium charcoal, to keep water from smelling "off."

3. Add more pebbles and then place 3 bulbs on top, root-side down, almost touching each other.

4. Add enough tepid water just touching the bottom of the bulbs. Refill when the water level falls by ¼ inch.

Paperwhites grow tall (16-20") and often tip over. Placing bulbs low in a tall container helps support the plants. You can also add short bamboo sticks to support the plants as they grow.

Another trick? The scientists at Cornell University discovered that you can add a diluted alcohol solution to the water to stunt the growth of the plant while the flowers remain large. Remember, moderation in everything, and while you have it out, toast the season and the beautiful flowers you'll soon enjoy!

Helpful Hints

How-To Sprout

So many of these activities for us involve participation with where food comes from: collecting chicken eggs, picking raspberries for dessert every evening in August after dinner, planting, watering, mounding, and harvesting potatoes, butchering elk, collecting and eating wild plants. ~ Kevin T.

1. Start with a large mouth mason jar, metal jar ring, cheese cloth to fit the mouth, and seeds to sprout. Alfalfa and broccoli are good starters and packed with nutrients!

2. Add 1 tablespoon of seeds and cover with lukewarm water. Secure cheese cloth over jar with the metal ring. Soak overnight.

3. The next day, leave cheesecloth on and drain the water into the sink, keeping seeds in the jar. Rinse seeds with clean water and drain out water. Place jar in a dark pantry or closet.

4. Rinse seeds with lukewarm water 2x daily.

5. After 3-4 days or when sprouts are 2 inches long, place them in a sunny window. Once they turn green (about 1 day), they will be ready to eat.

6. Place the sprouts in the jar in the fridge. They will be good for about 1 week. Enjoy in salads, sandwiches or pinchfuls!

Create a Museum! We collect numerous treasures. What do you do with them all?

- Display your items in large mason jars, a wooden niche display, on a mantel or shelf or in a special spot outside.

- Organize objects in different themes or categories.

- Create captions on bark, cloth and sticks, or with chalk.

- Invite guests to browse the collection or guide them through it.

- Rotate exhibits; keep precious items in a permanent collection.

Observation Station

1. Identify a spot in your home that inspires observation. Examples: it has a good view, it faces a bird feeder or thermometer.

2. Fill that place with tools that are always accessible: field guides, binoculars, scope, pencils, journal or clipboard.

3. Record notes in a journal. Include the time, date, weather and a sentence about the day (birthdays, the arrival of a special visitor, etc).

With all this data, create your own backyard field guide. Share, display, research, ask more questions and continue to observe!

Projects

• **Start a moon journal.** How does it change nightly?

• **Make your own feeder!** Cover a pinecone with peanut butter and seeds. Experiment with different seeds and "glue." Observe the activity: What birds boss around others? What birds co-exist? What happens when a stuffed animal is left at the feeder (or your cat!)?

• **Print a photo looking west from your home** (or draw a picture). Mark the location of the setting sun on the horizon daily or weekly. Notice seasonally how it sets north or south of due west. How would it look in a different latitude or hemisphere?

Pet Guides

One morning after a snowfall, my daughter and I found a set of tracks outside. Upon inspection we determined which direction they were headed and followed their meanderings around the yard. We found a bit of urine and pawing at a small clump of sage. The most exciting discovery: a spot where they intersected with tiny bird tracks and wing drags in the snow, a clear sign of flight. A thrilling story of survival unfolded before us; we just had to let the cat guide!

Caretaking Life Indoors

Compost is a big deal in our house. We talk a lot about the cyclical nature of organic waste to soil to new plants. Our kids help us recycle and where to put different types of garbage. ~ Kyla L.

1. Layer 2" of gravel into the bottom of a 1-quart wide mouth canning jar.

2. Fill the jar ¾ full with damp garden soil: not too wet and not too dry. Sprinkle it with a bit of water if necessary.

3. Mix a small handful of dead leaves into the top of the soil and sprinkle a bit more water if the leaves are dry.

4. Dig up a handful of worms from outside or buy red worms online. Add your worms to the jar.

5. Cover the mouth of the jar with a piece of cloth material to allow for air flow. A piece of an old t-shirt works great. Secure the material over the mouth of the jar with the metal canning ring.

6. Place the worm jar in a dark place.

7. Periodically, add more dry leaves and sprinkle water on dry soil.

Worms are wild creatures. Treat them kindly! Release them to a nice, new garden home after you have observed them for a few days. They will be a gift to your soil!

Observe

Notice the worm tunnels on the edge of the glass. Can you tell which way the worms are moving? What happens if you shine a flashlight on the jar? Do they have personalities? Give your worms names or tell a story about your worms. This helps us connect with and build empathy towards other animals.

Outside In

How do you bring the lessons of nature inside?

We moon-watch through skylights at night. ~ Tina F.

Our sunroom overlooks fields and a pond. We keep our binos and field guide close by and have a winter bird journal. ~ Tom M.

We create special "nests" for our guinea pig pets and constantly reference their wild relatives to explain their behavior (why they like cover, why they squeak, etc). ~ Lisa L.

Catch tadpoles and watch them turn into frogs at home. ~ Ruth B.

We observed butterfly metamorphosis in an indoor habitat. The kids dictated a daily journal which I typed, and they illustrated. ~ Dwight T.

Leaf rubbings and nature collages with LOTS of glue. ~ Renee R.

Bring nature treasures indoors: create art projects, display them on windowsills and even wrap them up as presents. ~ Sondi K.

Our preschoolers love collecting firewood—heck they love collecting lots of treasures while outdoors! ~ Jody C.

We study weather on the Grand Teton each day at the same time, and then take a picture to show the variation in the sunsets, from dust, rain, clouds, nearby fires, etc. ~ Robin W.

Take It Anywhere

Apply the Let the Kid Guide approach to any situation

Whether in the kitchen, in the car or in a fine arts museum, remember the Let the Kid Guide basics. Take a deep breath, use aspects of the The Huddle to smooth transitions, and return to the Roots of the approach to move forward gracefully, joyfully.

The Roots

Be playful and tune-in. Talk less and do more. Answer with questions. Model wonder and gratitude. These mantras get us through the day.

Road Trip

Modern day road trips are a far cry from sweating bullets on the hot, sticky seats of a station wagon, listening to a static-filled radio station. It's easy to plug kids into screens, and sometimes we must. However, you can break up electronic use. Challenge your tribe to a license plate or alphabet hunt. Create other scavenger hunts: each person makes their own before the trip and challenges the rest of the group on the road. Let kids answer, "Are we there yet?" Give them a paper map to follow. Use an atlas to draw a picture of each state. Look up state birds or other facts and record in a journal. Play the classic game of 20 Questions. Sing songs and make up lyrics with place-based words. Compose a group story, each person contributing one sentence. Go around until it naturally ends, usually in gut-busting laughter.

Museum

It might seem crazy to take a bunch of kids to a fine arts museum, but you can do it! This is how we set up for success: Check the museum's website. Preview the art, create scavenger hunts, or talk about the art. A little prior knowledge goes a long way to up curiosity and anticipation. Day of we get in the right frame of mind by asking what jobs involve art skills. We choose professions and assume the roles. Our mission? Find items or exhibits to help us in our jobs. This elevates engagement and purpose at the museum. We clearly write our first names and jobs on nametags. Then proudly enter and visit the information desk to introduce ourselves and ask about exhibits pertinent to our jobs. Docents are tickled by the exercise. Our jobs drive exploration. Success!

Quick Finds & Fun

- artwork of interest
- do a scavenger hunt
- match art to colors on a paintchip
- pose like a sculpture & take a photo with it
- caption a portrait - what is it saying?
- tell the story of a piece of art or draw it and mimic the style

Where else can you Let the Kid Guide?

- Standing in a seemingly endless line ~ model curiosity.
- Collaborating with a group at work ~ talk less and do more.
- Doing yard work ~ model wonder and gratitude.
- Waiting for a sibling to finish an activity ~ be playful.
- Visiting a new place ~ answer with questions.
- Walking to the bus stop ~ tune-in.
- Where else? You tell us!

Thank You!

We could not have done this project without you.

We offer this book as a collection of voices from our village. We all guide each other to live well and be well. From our tenacious friends and colleagues who trek into remote mountains with their children, find the wonder in sidewalk cracks and the joy in everything, to our mentors who share countless ideas, research and perspective, which have informed our approach, and the many people in between, this book is of and for you.

We are grateful to early sounding boards for their critical advice and feedback: Ruth Berkowitz, Laura Haspela, Roger Pasquier and Lisa Lowenfels. We are humbled by the support of Dr. Thomas Lovejoy and Ellen Haas, whose instant belief in this project provided us with confidence and clarity in purpose. Thank you to our Collective Wisdom contributors who provided numerous tips, tricks and tales. The initial design and layout of this book was developed by our friend Jodi Hougard Petty, who believes in the approach and lives it with her family. For this we give much thanks. Lastly, we'd like to thank our families who encourage, support, spark (and sometimes simply endure!) our enthusiasm for adventure, connection and being outside.

All of these people inspire us, and together we hope to inspire you to pack your bags, get out the door and let the kid guide.

The story's not over!
Keep in touch and share your triumphs and trip-ups with us.

Lisa and Margot

#letthekidguide
#letsgetout
letthekidguide.com

"If I have seen further than others,
it is from standing upon the
shoulders of giants."

~ Sir Isaac Newton

Our Guides

Inspiration for the Let the Kid Guide Approach

Let the Kid Guide was not built alone. In addition to our familiy and friends, numerous educators, doctors and artists greatly influence our work. We are reminded daily of the gifts that these "Guides" have given us. With humility and respect, we share a list of the foundation of the Let the Kid Guide approach.

Joseph Cornell

Sharing Nature: Nature Awareness Activities for All Ages

Perhaps one of the most beloved nature activity guides, a book that guided us early in our careers, is Cornell's "Sharing Nature." It includes accessible activities for every occasion that have been field-tested, for four decades! Plan ahead to find the perfect match to your outdoor adventure, or just toss it into your bag (it's a packable size!). Grab and flip to any page for an activity to capture any teachable moment. Forever fun. Forever relevant.

Kim John Payne, M.Ed.

Simplicity Parenting

Internationally renowned family consultant, Payne guides parents to reclaim childhood by taking practical steps to streamline the home environment, establish rhythms, create breaks in the schedule and scale back media. His simple recommendations are a salve for the busier, faster life, which pressures many of us as well as our children. Payne helps us hone our home environments to facilitate meaningful connection with our children.

David Sobel, M.Ed.

Wild Play: Parenting Adventures in the Great Outdoors

A pioneer in place-based education, Sobel was an early contributor and now authority on the movement. Many recent studies and research in neuroscience and psychology have recently caught up to his ideas: there is no substitute for hands-on experience, local projects and nurturing a child's innate sense of place in order to nurture his/her emotional health, increase engagement and performance in school, and cultivate active citizens. While participating in these types of projects, students learn essential core concepts across the disciplines, as well as critical problem-solving and social skills. In Sobel's most recent book, we meet his family, and through the lens of father and professor, he shares developmentally appropriate and tested ways to further connect children to their place. The place-based education movement is stronger for his decades-long commitment to and promotion of these studies and practices.

Jon Young, Ellen Haas & Evan McGown

Coyote's Guide to Connecting with Nature

Gifted storytellers and guides, Young, Haas and McGown are respected leaders of the wilderness awareness movement. "Coyote's Guide" is a comprehensive resource for mentors, educators and parents who understand the importance and timeliness of awareness, belonging and connection with nature. This guide is chock-full of activities, games, stories and inspiration, which ignite curiosity, playfulness and discovery. The games in this book have become favorites in our families and within the communities of students we teach.

Rachel Doorley, M.A.

Tinkerlab: A Hands-on Guide for Little Inventors
Doorley, a classroom and museum educator with a Masters in Arts Education from Harvard, sets the stage for creativity by providing an "invitation:" ready materials, a dedicated space and an emotionally safe space for her children to experiment, play and create with various materials. In addition to providing many great ideas for tinkering with your kids, this book makes us think of how we invite our kids and those we teach into a physical and mental space for exploration and learning. Doorley's anecdotes, research and activities support creative thinking, open-ended discovery, experimentation, process over product and "a fail-forward mindset, key for children and grown-ups alike!" We have brought the idea of tinkering into the field, on our road trips and in our kitchens. We invite you to tinker away!

Richard Louv

Last Child in the Woods
Louv coined the term "Nature Deficit Disorder" and explains, "The children and nature movement is fueled by this fundamental idea: the child in nature is an endangered species, and the health of children and the health of the Earth are inseparable." He backs his convictions with cutting-edge studies that link the plagues of the modern child - obesity, attention deficit disorder, and depression - with a lack of time outside. Louv's work affirms what we've witnessed in the field and creates a sense of urgency, as educators and parents, to do the work we do.

Carol S. Dweck, Ph.D.

Mindset: The New Psychology of Success

In her acclaimed book, Stanford University psychologist Dweck outlines why people succeed and how to foster success. Her work has popularized the use of terms fixed and growth mindset, empowering all of us to take control of our mindset in order to actualize our best selves. Teaching a growth mindset creates motivation and productivity, something we have used with our students as well as our own children. It has also challenged us to reflect on ourselves. In what situations do we exhibit a fixed mindset and in what situations do we exhibit a growth mindset? Why? What mindset do we want to model for our children? We need to walk the talk for our kids.

Patty Wipfler & Tosha Schore, M.A.

Listen: Five Simple Tools to Meet Your Everyday Parenting Challenges

Listen helps us understand our children's emotional outbursts and ease the stress of parenting in these difficult moments. Wipfler and Schore assist parents to identify not only the child's triggers, but also those of parents, and give practical tools for mitigating those triggers. One concept, "special time," we regularly incorporate into our practice; it allows parents and children to sink into their time together to cultivate a true sense of connectedness. Over and over we are drawn to these simple tools both with our own children and the students with whom we work in the classroom and field.

Lenore Skenazy

Free-Range Kids: How to Raise Safe, Self-Reliant Children

We've all been in the grocery store, with a screaming kid, feeling like we're being judged by everyone around us. Well, we haven't been quite as vilified as "America's worst mom," who has raised confident and competent, self-reliant kids. A journalist who has extensively researched the data behind actual risks to our children versus the urban myths (News flash: No kid has actually been poisoned by Halloween candy!), Skenazy encourages her kids to take calculated risks, when they are ready. Her meticulous research, approachable writing style and hilariously human stories, help affirm and support those of us muddling through the murky waters of parenting. Thank you, Lenore!

Bryd Baylor

I'm in Charge of Celebrations

Arizona writer Bryd Baylor influenced our teaching styles from the beginning and continues to inspire our parenting adventures. Her stories highlight the deep connection between the land and its people. *I'm in Charge of Celebrations, The Way to Start a Day, Everybody Needs a Rock, The Other Way to Listen,* among others, share with the reader values reinforced by the natural world: the importance of simplicity, the web of connections, and the delicate balance among all creatures, values we sometimes forget in our busy, often disconnected, lives.

Lisa Kosglow
Co-Author

Rooted in the Columbia River Gorge in Oregon, Lisa is an outdoor educator and owner of Let's Get Out summer camps. Her programs specialize in fostering a love of wild places, cultivating a sense of wonder and learning outdoor skills that last a lifetime. She is a Leave No Trace instructor and co-author of *Kidding Around the Gorge: The Hood River Area's Ultimate Guide for Family Fun,* 3rd Edition. In her past life, Lisa represented the United States on the U.S. Olympic Snowboard Team in 1998 and 2002. She coached both kids and adults in snowboarding on and off for over 10 years. She leads by example and shares her passion, drive and personal ethic--a true community guide.